MEMOS TO SOCIETY

WORDS ARE VERY EXPENSIVE

J A M E S   D A V I S

authorHOUSE®

AuthorHouse™
1663 Liberty Drive
Bloomington, IN 47403
www.authorhouse.com
Phone: 1 (800) 839-8640

Published by AuthorHouse 12/12/2017

ISBN: 978-1-5462-2039-8 (sc)
ISBN: 978-1-5462-2098-5 (e)

Print information available on the last page.

Introduction....

Words are the beginning of the meaning.

Its not the cost of the words, but value of its meaning.

James M Davis

ALMOST.......

Is soon enough.

AREN'T YOU LISTING?

I heard you, but I wasn't listing.

AFTER......

Is before it was.

AFTER TODAY.....

There will be another Tomorrow.

A STALKER.....

Age is creeping up upon you.

APPEARANCE.....

Appearing stupid, and acting dumb.

ALREADY......

Was here before.

ALRIGHT........

Is in good hands.

AFTER THE FACT.......

That's when it all started.

AND......

And is, and what was.

ALL IS NOT LOST......

Who loses that?

ANOTHER DAY......

Its just another day.

Its not the same as the other days.

ACCOUNTABLE......

How much do that cost?

ALL THE WAY......

Is not far enough.

ATOMIC BLAST......

Is a blast from the past.

AFTER ALL THE LOVE IS GONE.......

How do I find it?

How do I get it back?

Respect it.

A LOVE THAT I LOST......

Where did it go?

ALL I CAN GET.......

Is none of what you need.

ADDRESS......

From the Earth you came, and from the Earth you shall return..

ALONG THE WAY.......

What path are you taking, for such along way?

AGAIN......

When did that happen?

ALL......

How many is that?

ANYMORE......

How come?

AFFIRMATIVE ACTION........

Is that affirmed or not?

ADMIT......

James Davis

Who?

AVERAGE.....

Don't devalue your yourself !

AT THIS MOMENT......

How long do I have to wait?

AMOUNT......

Is it less then the cost?

A AIR OF CONSPIRACY......

It was wind aided.

AIN'T KNOW ROOM......

Well, stop taking up space.

ADIOS.....

Know time like the present.

BROKEN.......

Who broke the break?

Ask broken.

BACK WHERE IT WAS AT.......

It was never at where it was suppose to be at.

And where was that at?

BACK IN THE OLDEN DAYS.......

What's new about that?

BACKGROUND......

You miss the front.

BURDEN OF PROOF......

What kind of lies are they tell now?

BRAINSTORM.......

The tempest.

Cam before the storm.

BACK THE WAY YOU CAME......

I came the back way.

BITTERNESS......

You have a acquire taste within you.

BIZARRE.......

Your personality complements your personage.

BLABBERMOUTH......

Infectious.

BLAB......

Singing a Melody.

BLANK.......

Don't try to think, because theirs

nothing there.

BLEAK.......

Your heart is just as bleak as your mind.

BLACKMAIL.....

Don't extort yourself.

BLESSING......

Blessing are given not ask for.

BLEEDING HEART,.......

Is a crying heart.

BLIP......

Is that all your mind can contain?

BLUEBLOOD.....

What happen to the Red?

BLUEPRINT.....,

Mapping out your stupidity.

BLUFF.......

Be careful what you wish fore.

BONDAGE.......

Held without bail.

BOOZE.......

Happy liquor.

BORDERLINE......

Watch your step !

BOGGLE THE MIND......

If you let it.

Oh !

Never mind !

BOISTEROUS.......

Is that all you have say?

BONA- FIDE.....

I am legitimate as they come.

BRAINWASH.....

It all depends on what your using.

BODACIOUS......

The 8th wonder of the world.

BORING......

A dull situation.

BORN AGAIN......

With renew Faith.

BOTHER.......

You'll beg the Dead.

COULD.......

Ask could if I could?

CAN'T......

Ask can't if I could?

CAN.....

Can can't can?

CAD.......

You are what you are.

CALLOUS......

You have low grade personality.

CAMOUFLAGE.....

You can't hide something that you

don't have. A moral compass.

COMPREHENSION.......

I can explain it to you, but it might

take you sometime to comprehend.

CANDOR......

Your lies complements your candor.

COMPLETE.....

Your reasons and reasoning are

incomplete.

COMPATIBLE......

Your ignorance is compatible with your stupidity.

COMPROMISE.....

You can't compromise with Ignorance.

CLEAN......

Your dirty in a clean kind of way.

CITATION......

Your being cited for your asinine personality.

CAUGHT......

Caught by ignorance, and jailed for stupidity.

CAPTIVITY.....

Held against their well.

COPY......

Duplicating ignorance.

CORNERSTONE.......

who laid the foundation?

COHORT......

If you cohort with fool's

you'll be come one.

COMBINATION.....

We are safe in numbers

COMBATANT......

Stop fighting yourself, you'll never win.

compromise.

CODE.....

I will not give up my badge of honor.

COHERENT.......

Slow down. I read you loud and clear.

Stop being so incoherent.

COLLATERAL DAMAGE......

And that to shall past,

COMPETE.......

Incompetency is your way of life.

COLLAPSE......

If you don't stand for something,

you'll fall for anything.

COMMENT......

I want to add or take away.

No !

Comment.

CASUALTY.......

Friendly Fire.

CATCH.....

Caught it !

CAVERNOUS......

Your Mind.

CREATION.......

Innate.

COINCIDENCE......

James Davis

Its never to late.

DONE........

Done is never done.

Lets do it.

DOWN AND OUT......

I must dig my way out.

DO WHAT YOU WANT.......

What do want want to do?

DON'T DO THAT......

Because, that don't do that.

DID BEFORE......

Before didn't.

DON'T KNOW.

Don't knew it.

DIDN'T COME......

Ask came.

DIG......

Hey Man, dig this?

You ! dig it.

DEEP DOWN......

That's where its at !

DOWN......

You grow up .

Than you go down.

Quoting.... What goes up must go down.

Return !

DOES.....

Do does know?

DO WHAT YOU CAN........

That's never done.

Can, can do !

DOWN TO THE BONE......

Where is the meat?

DEEP WITHIN......

You can't live without it.

DIRECTION.......

Follow Jesus.

DEFECTOR......

Abscond from reality.

DOOR.......

Close them behind you.

DOWN TIME......

Up- grade it.

DIVIDE......

Equally.

DON'T DO IT.......

Don't does what it do.

DOWN THE HILL.....

Who came up the hill first, Jack or Jill?

DISGRUNTLED......

Frustration with oneself.

DISGUISE........

Face it !

DISGRACE......

Honor it.

DISHONEST......

Are you surprise?

DISINFECT YOURSELF......

Don't miss a spot,

DISTORT......

Don't resort to distort.

DISTRIBUTE......

Give as much as you get.

DISQUALIFY.....

You must Qualify first.

DISPUTE.....

Freedom of speech.

EVERLASTING......

Faith in Jesus.

EVER......?

Of course.

EVERYBODY......

Is everyone.

EACH......

Equal parts.

ECHELON......

I am find where I am at.

EDIFICE......

The vision of GOD.

EAGER......

Your wasting time.

ELAPSE......

Mind is a terrible thing to waste.

EJECTION......

Your fired.

EGOTISM......

Where did you find that at?

ELECT......

SELECT.

ELDER.......

Older than I.

ELATED.....

Beyond happiness.

EARS.......

Are for listing to what you've you have heard.

EMBEZZLE......

Taking thing for granted.

ELUDE......

False identity.

EMBED......

Your impaled in Me.

ELOPE

Abscond.

ENERGIZE......

A spark.

ENTER......

Why?

EVERMORE......

A nothing less.

ERUPT.......

Boiling over.

EVALUATE......

Taking notice.

DEVELOP......

Manifest.

EMERGENCY.....

The Urgency Room.

ELIMINATE......

Dispose off.

EYEWITNESS.....

Did you see that?

No !

I saw what you Witness.

EXTRINSIC.....

You a universal personality.

EXTROVERT......

Stay where you are.

Your just find.

EYESORE.....

Is your your own reflection.

FORGO.....

Is long gone.

FORK IT OVER.......

I am using a spoon.

FOR WHAT......

What is, for what?

FABLES......

True or consequences.

FACADE......

Something is not right.

FACE......

Some just can't face it.

FACETIOUS......

Whats so not funny?

FADE......

Some do and some don't.

FAILURE.....

Failure is an option.

Don't.

FAIL- SAFE......

How can you do that?

Fall - safe.

FALSEHOOD......

Take it off...... The Hood.

FAKE......

Whats so original about that?

FALL - GUY.......

Oh !

He was pushed.

FOLLOW......

Where did it go?

FAR-OUT......

That's still to close.

FEW GOOD MEN......

Don't forget to count the Women.

FARSIGHTED......

Is that what I See?

FINISH......

Finish is never done.

FEISTY.......

You better save some for later.

FAR-REACHING.....

Are you sure you can hold on?

FETCH.......

Is it worth retrieving?

FOR ONCE.....

Easier said than done.

FOR NOW !

Can't for now wait for later?

FOR EVER MORE......

How is that go to last?

FAR-LESS......

Could be far worst.

FAR AND BETWEEN......

Its far and between the middle.

FUMIGATE.....

Clean your Soul.

FUGITIVE.....

You keep running away, Why.

FORE-CLOSE.....

James Davis

Before you do that.

FRUSTRATION......

Is when you don't listen too yourself.

GRAMMAR......

Little talk.

GANG RELATED......

We are not relatives.

GROUND BREAKING.......

Don't get caught.

GOOD AS IT GETS......

When I'm I going to get some?

GRAND-VIEW.......

I know !

GOVERNMENT.......

Is it that what it suppose to be?

GUIDE......

Me?

Your the one who can't see for looking.

GOING OUT OF MY MIND......

How come? Why? And what for?

GROWING PAINS......

How old are they?

GRANDSTAND......

Get off the stage.

GROUND HOG DAY......

Who's cooking it?

GIVING UP......

Ho No !

I'm going up !

GUARDING.......

How can you be guarding me, when your under-guard?

GUIDELINE......

Do you walk them, or do you cross them?

GET ENOUGH......

How much is that?

GIVE IT SOME TIME......

Wait broke the wagon.

GIVE IT BACK.......

I want mind up front.

GAVE......

Have you ever gave to the given?

GATHERING......

A Family Reunion.

GOING AND COMING

Your back already?

GROUND ZERO......

Nothing there.

GRIEVANCE......

Have a grievance with yourself,

not with Me.

GOT TO BE......

Never that !

GOING TO BE.....

Hoping that !

GIVE SOMETHING THAT YOU NEVER GAVE.....

Yourself.

GREAT......

Great is before greatness.

You become great at the

being.

Greatness become everlasting.

GIANTS......

They are smaller than you think.

GAIN.....

How much did I gain?

You gain what you lost.

GHETTO.......

A Concentrate Camp......

GROUNDLESS......

No foundation.

HABITATION.....

Is your plot.

HALFHEARTED......

I'll save the best for last.

HALITOSIS.......

Silence.is golden.

HOW?

Try it !

HOUSE......

A coat.

HARD TO SAY.....

What's so easy about being to hard?

HOW MUCH.....

To little.

HOW CAN I?

I can.

HOW MUCH IS A HALF OF A HALF?

A half of a whole.

HOSTAGE.....

Someone I do know.

HE WOULDN'T DO THAT.......

He did it.

HISTORY.....

Follow it.

Catch it.

HAVE A BALL......

Play with it.

HAVING SOMETHING TO SAY.....

But not much to talk about.

HAVING TOO LOOK......

I already saw what I seen with my sight.

HOW IS EVERYONE?

Are you asking me, or you telling me.

HARD.....

Its hard when its easy.

HALF OF TO MUCH......

Is to much of nothing.

HALF OF NOTHING.....

Is a part of something.

HOW CAN YOU TELL?

By asking.

HUNT......

I caught myself.

HALF OF MAN.......

The other half is catching up.

HOW MUCH TIME DO WE HAVE.......

Time enough.

HEAVEN MUST BE LIKE THIS.......

Somethings never change.

HOW DO A PERSON FIND WHAT THEY HAVE LOST?

Go back the same way they came.

HOW DO I BEAT HIM......

Join him.

HEMORRHAGING.....

Close your mouth.

HEAD-START......

Where would that be?

At the beginning or at the start?

HIS......

Its not his or his.

SO HOW IS IT?

What it was.

IDEALIST......

Dream Merchant.

IDENTICAL......

The opposite, but the same.

IDENTITY.....

False impression.

IGNORAMUS.....

you are at the top of the list.

IDENTIFY......

Identify yourself, find out who you really are.

ILL-SUITED.......

You wear it well.

I DO NOT......

Why?

IGNORE.....

Excuse yourself.

INJURED.....

Mentally.

IF.....

And?

I'M NOT.

Who said you were?

I MIGHT BE......

You were born to be.

INCREASE......

You went beyond and below.

You went too far.

INTELLIGENT OFFICER.....

what if is was a dumb one?

IT.....

How do you know?

IDOL WORSHIPERS.....

False pretense

IT WILL BE.......

If you let it.

I KNEW IT......

But how did know knew it.

INFAMOUS......

This is your 15 minutes of fame.

Infamous.

INFLATE.....

Your just blowing in the wind.

INCOMING.....

Your so out going.

INCREDIBLE.....

Amazing grace.

INCOGNITO.....

Why the Mask?

INFLATED......

Your ego.

IN THE NICK OF TIME.....

Who is Nick?

I AM NOT WHO I AM.....

Who where you than.

I AM NOT TRYING TO STOP YOU.......

I am trying to hold you.

ITS YOU....

No !

Its Me !

I am sorry......

I am not !

I KNOW WHO THAT IS.......

Who?

The one I thought it was.

I CAN'T HELP IT......

I am helpless.

I NEED......

I know what you need,

and, you needed. to need.

ITS FOREVER.....

That's never gone.

JAIL.....

For condemn SOULS.

JUDGE......

That's all they do..

JUST AS MUCH......

Or more of the same.

JUST CAUSE......

Or a cause for justice.

JUST US.....

Why not them?

Because their not Us.

JUST YOU......

Who me?

Is that you?

JANITOR......

Its a dirty job, someone has to do it.

JAUNDICED.......

Is it just on your back?

JET-SET......

Broke the sound barrier.

JOINT.....

Up in smoke.

JOLT.......

Electrifying.

JACK BE NIMBLE JACK BE QUICK .

JACK JUMPED OVER THE CANDLE STICK.

Why did he do that?

Because he was nimble.

JIMMY......

You can't have the key to my heart, now you want

too Jimmy it.

JOINT ACCOUNT.......

Whats you is mine.

JUNK.....

Something old, and something new.

JOURNAL.....

Remembering what you said to yourself.

JOKER......

Its not funny any more, Why?

JOURNALIST......

Who you report too?

JOLLY......

Happy days are again.

Joyful !

JOKE.......

Its not funny any more.

WHY?

JUNIOR......

A Man and half.

JUMBO.....

Heavy Love !

JUST......

That's the way it should be.

JUSTICE OF THE PEACE......

Is that all it is?

JUNK FOOD......

What yard is that in?

JUVENILE DELINQUENT......

He's also tardy.

JUNGLE......

Its Jungle out there.

Dark Too.

JOSTLE......

I'll tell you what.

You take the high road and I'll take

the low road.

jilt.....

you have a Jolt coming.

JOG.....

Come.

Lets Run !

KEEN......

It still need to be always sharped.

KEPT.......

Kept, kept keep.

Well,who kept kept?

KICK BACK......

I wasn't kicking the first time.

KILL JOY......

Why would you do something like that?

KIND.....

Where did you find that at?

In kindness.

KIND HEART......

Kind heart, lost Soul.

KEY......

It opens up new and old problems.

KNOW HOW......

How did they know that?

KNOW IT ALL......

Know it all, don't know all of that.

KILL.....

Who murdered that?

KNOCK IT OFF......

Its easier said then done.

KNOCK OFF.....

Who?

KEEP THINKING ABOUT YOUR THOUGHTS.....

Its like being without Wisdom and looking for Wise.

See, you can't have one without the other.

Because you thoughts are always thinking.

KEEP ON PUSHING......

It will make you stronger.

KIND OF MAN.....

Man kind.

KIND OF WOMAN......

She IS !

KEEP THAT SOME OLD FEELING.....

Don't pawn it.

KWANZAA....

Thanks for given.

KEEP GOING......

Follow your destiny, don't let it

follow you.

KISS......

A Introduction.

KEY WITNESS......

Unlock the truth.

KNEEL.....

Kneel for a friend and blow for the crowd.

KNOWN QUANTITY......

Absent of Quality.

KNUCKLE HEAD.......

Everybody know a fool when

we see but not when we are one.

KNOWLEDGE.....

Is all knowing.

KNOTS.....

Why are you ting yourself up?

KNOW......

Knew.

KNEW.......

Who knew it before know knew it?

KNOW WHO?

Who knew who?

KNACK......

You have knack for stupidity.

LAB.......

Working on a groovy thing.

James Davis

LABEL......

I have one you that fits you?

LABOR OF LOVE......

On the job training.

I am not going to retiring.

LABOR PARTY.......

When do it start?

LAG......

Your lagging in thoughts.

LADY LIKE......

Most Women Are.

LAME.......

Its all spreading through your mind.

LACKADAISICAL......

So what !

LASCIVIOUS......

Your mind is in the gutter.

LAST CHANCE.....

Is your first choice.

LASTING FOREVER......

Its a long way off.

LITTLE IS KNOWN......

But much is more.

LOSE.....

You lose it?

No !

I lost it.

LAST BUT NOT LEASE......

Lease is not the last of it.

LINK...

Did you find your missing link?

LETS NOT FORGET.......

What forgot

To forget?

LAPSE.....

How did it get that far?

LETS FIGURE THIS OUT?

Are going to Add or subtract?

A LIKE.....

Ask the same?

LIKE IT OR LEAVE IT......

Your going to leave what you like?

LETS NOT THINK ABOUT IT......

My thoughts already have.

LONG TIME COMING......

You better hurry up !

Your on borrow time.

YOUR LEAKING......

Inside and out.

LEARNING......

Your learning what you have learned.

LOVE ME OR LIKE ME......

Its your pick.

LEAN ON ME......

Who's holding you up?

LISTEN TO WHAT I SAY.....

I couldn't even hear that.

LAW BREAKER......

Its in pieces

THE LAST THING YOU WOULD EVER KNOW......

Is what you knew.

LAND FALL.....

Pick it up.

MORE......

And less of it.

MORE OF THE SAME......

I am tired more of the same.

Can I have more with the same?

MOST DAYS......

Is not enough for one.

MAY I?

Ask God !

MATTER OF FACT.......

Because the fact matters.

MORE OF SOME......

I want some that.

MUCH OF WHICH......

Some of it.

MOST OF IT......

Its some of the most of it.

MOST OF THE HALF.......

How can you get most of a half,

when the most is more than a half?

MUCH BETTER......

What can be better than that?

More better.

MUCH MORE......

What do you want?

Much of it or more of it?

Or much of the more?

MOBILE......

Your on the Run.....

THE BEST OF IT......

The best is yet to come.

Look for it.

MORE THAN MEETS THE EYES......

Sight.

MEET......

Connection.

MISSING......

Everything that I need.

MORE MONEY.......

That's less Cents.

MOST OF YOU......

Is a part of Me.

MAKE......

Its already Made.

MOST OF NOTHING......

Is all of something.

MAKING SOMETHING NEW.....

From something from Old.

MADE TO ORDER.......

Who made you do that?

MADE IN THE BEGINNING.....

That's a start.

MAYBE......

That's better than nothing.

MEANS MUCH.....

There is much meaning to Much.

MELT DOWN......

Mold Him.

MASTERS......

That's what their there for.

NAKED.....

When I was born.

NEVER.....

Is for forever.

NEXT......

Which next?

There is more then one.

NONE......

Its better then nothing.

NOTHING PERSONAL.....

But it is what it is

NOTHING WRONG.....

How many right do you need.

NOT NOW......

When is that going to be?

NO WAY OUT.....

Well, how did you find your way In?

NOTHING CAME BEFORE OR AFTER.....

It came together.

NOTHING CAN COME OF IT.......

I already came.

NEXT TIME.....

Time first never the next.

NOT TRUE......

Well, what is?

TRUTH !

NOTHING GOOD CAN COME OUT OF THIS.....

It has already.

The bad is gone.

And that's a good thing.

NOTHING BUT THE REAL THING.....

What's wrong with that?

Nothing !

NO WAY......

How did it get that way?

What way?

The way it always been.

NOW IS ENOUGH....

When is enough is enough?

When its not enough.

NO IT WON'T WORK.....

(It will).

NICE.....

Nice isn't either.

NEED HELP !

Help yourself.

NO! I AM NOT READY......

Neither is ready.

NOR......

I can ignore that.

NOISELESS.......

Noise without sound.

NEXT THING.......

The thing nothing knew.

Was known.

NOMAD......

I founded my way.

NEIGHBOR.......

The one who is always peeping out the window.

NARROW......

Minded.

NATIVE......

Instinctual.

NAMELESS.....

Living without a Face.

NAPPY......

So is yours.

NAME BRAND.....

Off brand.

NAVIGATE.....

Follow the fellow brick road.

OFTEN......

That's plenty.

Plenty is often enough.

OPINION.......

They both have one.

OPPOSITE.....

They are the same.

OCTOBER......

Indian Summer.

Who else was there?

OBSESS....

With nothing.

OAF.....

That's you.

OUT GOING......

There's no more left in you.

OLD BOY......

Young Man.

ODOR......

You smell like you look.

ODDITY......

You look very familiar, Odd.

OCCULT.....

A ball of confusion.

OBLIQUE.....

Its your mind.

OCCASIONALLY.....

That's when you start to think.

OFF BASE......

Who's playing it?

OCCUPANT.....

Why do you let everyone occupy you?

OFF HANDED.....

He must be.

OF.....

What do he want?

OPPONENT......

Within yourself.

OPPRESS.....

Always keep your head up

OPTICAL.....

See within.

ORBIT......

That's why you can't concentrate.

ON GOING.....

Just keep moving.

ON COMING.....

Just keep going.

ON YOUR WAY......

Which way?

OPEN......

With caution.

OBSTINATE.....

That's why you can't communicate with yourself.

OBSERVE.....

Observe what you can't see.

OXYMORON......

What's so silly about that?

OWNER......

I am my own franchise.

ODD MAN OUT......

Watch what comes back In.

ODD FOLLOW.....

That's not rare.

PACE......

Keep up.

PACK......

Which one of you is following the leader?

PAGANS.......

They believe in themselves.

PAGE......

What page or life line are you on?

PAIN KILLER.......

Are you trying to commit suicide?

PALE......

You must of seen something that frighten you?

PAMPER......

Get over it.

PANHANDLE......

Are you right or left handed?

PANIC DISORDER......

Its not a disorder.

Its fear.

PACE MAKER......

That's what its for.

PAINLESS....

That's my kind of prescription.

PAIN FULL.....

Why couldn't I have it half full?

PACKING HOUSE......

Who's doing the unpacking?

PAD LOCK......

Will that lessen the blow?

PAIR.......

How many can you wear?

PROTOCOL.....

The right or the wrong thing to do.

PAPER CHASE.....

Who can run the fastest.

PROPER PLACE.......

Are you asking Me, or telling I?

PART TIME......

Part time unbalanced and full time

Simpleton.

PROPORTION......

A part of everything.

PICK ME UP......

You can do that yourself.

PLACES AND PACES.......

That's where their at.

PEOPLE WHAT DO YOU WANT FIRST?

The pieces or the parts?

Do the whole come with it?

PARTS OF MY PAST......

Are in pieces

PRIVATE......

You can't have that, it belongs to Me.

PEEPING TOM......

Those peeping tom's can't be trusted.

PEOPLE GET READY.....

Ready wasn't ready.

PAST TIME.....

I would rather walk with it.

POINT BLANK......

You need a live round.

PEACE OFFERING......

Can you afford it?

QUEER......

Strange but True.

QUACK.......

You never lied.

QUALIFIED......

Differently.

With a P. H. D; in stupidity.

QUIET......

Sure, as soon as you shut up.

QUICKER THAN YOU THINK......

My thoughts were quicker.

QUICKEN......

Who quicken it?

Quicker.

QUALITY CONTROL......

That's a must.

QUENCH.....

It all depends on favor.

QUARANTINE......

Your Mind is infected.

QUAINT......

Quite.

QUIT......

I don't have time.

QUESTIONABLE.....

Ask it?

QUANTIFY......

Can you?

QUARRY......

There's a Bulls Eye, on your back.

QUARTER......

Why don't you go all the way?

QUARTER HORSE.....

You get what you paid for.

QUARTER AFTER......

Why are you after that?

QUARTER BEFORE.......

Oh!

You can't wait?

QUEASY......

Your looks make me unease.

QUOTA......

You got more than you bargain for.

QUICK.....

Quick to learn and fast to act stupid.

QUAINT......

Is in your personality.

You fit and you wear it will.

QUALITY CIRCLE......

Is a qualified one.

QUADRUPLE......

You have 4 Faces of Even.

QUALM......

I must keep my eye's on you.

You make me so Nauseating.

QUIVER......

Don't even take me there !

QUIZ.....

Don't laugh, words are very expensive.

QUIP.....

This is the way you sound.

QUEST.....

It was teachable.

QUESTION-LESS......

Stuck on stupidity.

REST OF MY LIFE.....

Is all of it !

RUN WAY CHILD.......

I was wild before I ran.

ROUGH RIDER.......

It doesn't have to be that way.

ROUGH EDGES.....

Where did they come from?

REALLY WANT.......

But what do you really need?

ROCKY MORE.....

Rock steady.

RABBI......

Do he preach or teach?

RABBLE ROUSER....

Matter scatters.

RABID.....

Bitten by a Fool.

RAGE.....

From within.

RAGGED......

Sloppy personality.

RAGGED EDGE.....

A two headed sword.

You have a choice.

RAID.....

Leave my Heart along.

RAG TIME....

Party time.

REAL......

How come?

RAW.......

That's your Heart.

RECENT.......

Not now

REFILL.....

It was un-empty.

RETURN......

A bout face.

RIVAL....

You can't be like Me, or be Me.

ROAD BLOCK.....

Obstructionist.

RATHER......

Rather now, not later and not soon.

READY TO WEAR......

Ready rolled.

REACT......

That's impossible when your brain dead.

RECOIL.....

Why are doing this to yourself?

REMOVE......

Means to withdraw from removal.

REFRAIN......

But, still hold on.

REFUTE......

Prove it.

REFORM.....

How can you, when you don't know how?

Show Me !

REFUSE.....

I won't do it.

SHELTER........

Comfort.

SELF.......

What else do you need to know.

SUGGEST......

Did I ask for your opinion?

SHOULDN'T.......

I want you to meet can't.

STOP.......

Why I am going?

SURE......

Are you?

And how come?

STUN......

At yourself.

SINGLE......

Less than one.

SECRETE......

Untold Truth.

SURPRISE......

A rude awaking.

SHE......

Sh is Her.

SHOOT.....

Take the shot.

Someone else took it.

SAVING GRACE......

That's a excellent account.

SHIELD.......

Badge of honor.

SERVICE.....

Fix Me up.

SEA.......

A Big Bath Tub.

SELF SERVING.....

I don't mind if I do.

SHORT CUT.......

Lets split it in half.

SHOULD I?

Could you?

SEE......

Your looking for something that

you never saw.

SAW.....

You saw something that you never seen yet.

SHOUT.......

Say it loud.

SEVERAL......

Less than many.

SHOW ME......

Do you have a ticket?

STORM.......

Ask Clam.

SEW......

Stitch him up.

SAY SOMETHING......

You wasn't listing.

SOUNDS GOOD.....

Not bad.

STAY UP.......

Why?

Are you trying to take Me down?

TALL-TALE......

Short ending.

TELLING SOMETHING......

And let it, be told.

TO LATE.....

What time is it?

TO SMART......

Your smart enough to know,

that your not.

TELL ME.......

Tell me what you know and

I'll tell you how you knew.

TELL ME HOW......

And I'll tell you why.

THINGS HAPPEN......

That's what make the world go around

THINK......

I don't have have a thought.

THOUGHTS.......

I was just thinking.

TACKY.......

Look at you.

James Davis

TACT........

What away to go.

TACTICAL......

Desperate measures.

TAIL BACK.......

Look who's talking.

TAKE OFF.......

Its already on.

TAKE AWAY......

Give it back the same way.

TAKE DOWN.......

What's up !

TAKE OVER......

Someone already have.

TAKE UP......

Look up.

TOM THUMB......

What happen to your fingers?

TIME OUT.......

Ask time, if its alright.

TO BAD......

And that's not good.

TRYING TO GET MY LIFE BACK.......

What you need, an invention?

TALL ORDER.....

Short cook.

TREAT.......

If you act like that, you'll be treated that.

TOOK......

You took something that you didn't need.

TRENCH MOUTH......

Shut up !

TRESPASSING.....

You didn't even knock.

TRI COLOR......

Me, Myself, and I.

TRIFLING......

Who does that?

They do.

TRAIL.......

Your on your own.

TRICKERY.......

By your own hands.

TRICK.......

Are you?

TREMOR......

Are you afraid of yourself?

UMBILICAL CORD......

Tie it.

I have a life to Live.

UGLIFY......

Can you justify that.

UGLY.......

Is where Beauty hides.

UH.....

Uh-uh.

UNABLE......

But not disable.

UNTIL.....

Why do I have to wait for that?

UNKNOWN.....

Was never known.

UNHEARD OF.......

Of course.

You wasn't listing.

UNSURE.....

Sure enough.

UNCLEAN......

I have a lot of dirty on you.

ULTIMATUM.......

Take it, or leave it.

UNACCOMMODATING.....

Failure to respond.

UNACCOUNTABLE.....

There's more then you that meets the eye.

UNTAMED......

Wild thing.

UNRESPONSIVE.....

Don't have a clue.

URGENT......

Not soon enough.

UNHINGE.....

Your Mouth.

UNAVAILABLE.....

But visible.

UNINFORMED....

You wasn't missed inform.

UNSTABLE.....

You have a bad balancing act.

UNSOUND......

I can't hear, but I sure can listen.

UNSOPHISTICATED.....

What happen to your mask?

UN-BACKED....

Why is that?

UNBLESSED.....

Well, be damned.

UNBELIEF.....

You always was.

UNBECOMING.....

That's why you never came.

UNCIVILIZED.....

Grow out.

UNCLE SAM......

He already had Me !

UNCONSCIOUS......

You were !

UNCUT.....

I am worth it?

VITAL....

Can you see the signs?

VICTORY......

Its hard when your fighting against against yourself.

VISION.....

James Davis

It all depends on yours sight, and what your looking for.

VAGA-BOND.....

Squatter.

Do you mind if have a seat?

VAGRANT......

Where am I?

VICIOUS.....

Is how you treat yourself?

VACUOUS......

Is that you?

VALENTINE.....

Have a Heart.

VERMINOUS.......

You both look familiar.

VERTIGO......

You need a tune-up.

VACATION.......

Take one.

Give your mind a break.

Before it gets broken.

VACATE......

Your empty your shell, shed a new one.

VANITY.....

Am I worth it?

VAPID.......

You have know favor.

VARIOUS......

Your the same as yourself.

You can't help it. Help !

VEILED.....

Do you always hide from yourself?

VEGETATIVE STATE.....

Go organic.

VAULT......

Is my Heart.

VASTITUDE.....

The World is big enough for both of us.

Let share it?

VEER......

You have your own lane in life.

Don't veer into mine, someone could get hurt.

VELOCITY......

Take your time, you can't catch it.

VENALITY......

Are you that easy?

VENDIBLE.....

That road was taken once.

VENDETTA.....

Stop blaming your yourself.

Heal !

VENGEANCE......

Its not mine.

Its who's?

VENERATE.....

MYSELF !

VENOMOUS.....

Is your Heart.

VENTILATE.....

Your head is stuff.

It need Ventilation.

VERACIOUS......

What else can I say?

WHICH ONE......

That one.

Which one.

WERE YOU WHERE......

That's where I was.

WHAT DID YOU WANT?

Do I did?

WANT SOMETHING.......

That's what need.

WHAT'S GOING ON?

The same thing that went on.

WAG......

Look in the rear.

WAGE SCALE......

Why is it empty?

WATCHFUL THINKING.....

Who's keeping watch on thoughts?

WELL DONE......

Your not sticking me with know fork in Me.

WHAT CAN I DO FOR YOU?

Nothing !

Its what you can do for yourself.

Do that for Me !

WATCH OUT......

That's what I am looking for.

WHO CAN?

The one who couldn't.

WHAT?

Uh !

WHO COULDN'T?

The one who did.

WHAT'S ON YOUR MIND?

The same thing that's in it.

WELL TO DO.......

Well, how do you do that?

WHAT CAN HAPPEN?

Like it always has.

WHAT WILL HAPPEN?

Ask Murphy's Law.

WHAT DID HAPPEN?

What was done.

WHETHER YOU KNEW OR NOT......

How you didn't know what you knew?

WHAT WAS SAID?

Everything and nothing.

What part do you want to hear?

WHY CAN'T YOU UNDERSTAND?

Because I understood.

WHERE IS EVERYBODY?

Where you were.

WHICH WAY IS UP?

Where it suppose to be.

WHAT BECAME OF AN BROKEN HEART......

It healed itself.

WHAT'S WRONG WITH HIM?

He don't know.

WHY CAN'T I GO?

Because I don't know where I am going.

WHAT WILL TOMORROW BRING?

What it brought.

WE ARE ON OUR WAY......

Which way?

The same way we came.

X.....

I've been x-ed, x'd, x-ing, or x'ing.

X......

Its Me !

Sign, sealed, and delivered.

X......

Is that the spot?

What spot?

Where the **X** is?

??????

Y......

You !

YANK......

I'll yank your breath away.

YAWNER.....

Your boring every time I see you.

I yawn.

YEARNING.......

Fill me from top to bottom.

YELLOW BELLY.......

Their every where.

YOU'LL NO......

But, don't forget what you knew.

YOUNG.....

How can you be the youngest

without being the younger?

Which makes you the youngest out

of the younger, and makes young.

YOU AND I......

How did I happen to you?

YEAH......

Yep, goes with that yeah.

YOU AND THEY.......

Them, those, and they.

Is there any room us?

YET.......

Its coming.

YONDER......

Far and near.

Near as far as you can get.

YOUR CRAZY.......

At least I know.

YOU DIDN'T KNOW?

If knew did.

How didn't know didn't know?

YOU CAME BEFORE YOUR TIME.....

What took you so long?

YOU ARE NOT YOU......

I know.

I am I !

YOU DON'T HAVE A LEG TO STAND ON......

And you sure can't use mine.

YOUR ON YOUR OWN WAY......

Follow it.

YOUNG ADULT......

Not yet old.

YOUNGISH......

Not yet young.

YOUTH......

Neither.

YOURS TRULY......

Are you truly being truthful?

YOU'VE......

Yes I have.

Why?

Have you?

YOURSELF.......

I better Be.

YOUR TASTELESS......

Yucky.

YUP.......

Its not that important, but Yup !

YOUR TURN.....

Which way?

YOU HAVE ONE MOMENT......

I'll take it.

YOU CAN'T GO.......

Gone went with go.

YOU ALRIGHT?

What's wrong with that?

YOU CAN DO WHAT WANT.....

Or have what you need.

ZEALOUS.....

I am going for Gusto.

ZERO GRAVITY.......

You have know foundation.

ZERO SUM......

Less than nothing.

ZERO HOUR.....

I need more time. Time doesn't stop.

ZERO BASE

Your on your own.

ZONE.......

This is throne I call my own so don't

pee on the seat. Please be kind and look

behind and pick up the seat.

ZOO.....

I see a lot of familiar faces.

Printed in the United States
By Bookmasters